P9-BUH-171

Design: Art of Design
Recipe Photography: Peter Barry
Jacket and Illustration Artwork: Jane Winton, courtesy
of Bernard Thornton Artists, London
Editors: Jillian Stewart and Kate Cranshaw

CLB 3522
This edition published in 1994 by
Whitecap Books Ltd., 1086 West 3rd Street,
North Vancouver, B.C., Canada V7P 3JS
© 1994 CLB Publishing,
Godalming, Surrey, England.
All rights reserved
Printed and bound in Singapore
ISBN 1-55110-207-2

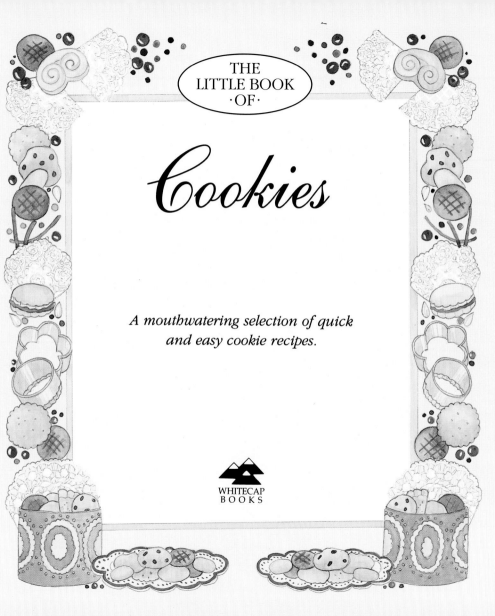

THE LITTLE BOOK ·OF·

Cookies

*A mouthwatering selection of quick
and easy cookie recipes.*

WHITECAP
BOOKS

Introduction

Tasty though they may be, bought cookies are no match for the homemade variety. Fresh from the oven, home-baked cookies crumble in the mouth, and have the good, wholesome flavor that all those chemical additives seem to obliterate in commercially made foods. Excellent, too, are home-baked savory crackers, which are particularly impressive at dinner parties.

Cookies are fun to experiment with and quite adaptable when it comes to making your own changes. Your own cookies do not have to be as sweet as bought ones, which are usually packed with sugar. Of particular interest to those following a low-cholesterol diet or one free of dairy products is the fact that you can choose the type of shortening used, and although butter is generally believed to give the best taste, margarines are an excellent substitute.

Most people are surprised at how easy and quick cookies are to make. It is just a matter of mixing the ingredients together, rolling out the dough and cutting the shapes, or simply putting spoonfuls of mixture onto a baking tray. And baking often takes less than 15 minutes. On those days when there are no cookies

in the cupboard, it can actually be quicker to make a quick batch than to go out and buy a packet. The smell of baking is wonderful, too, and in a houseful of children this will soon bring expectant faces around the kitchen table.

The rolling out and cutting of cookie shapes is a simple and satisfying activity, and one in which children love to help. Stars, crescents and novelty shapes all lend themselves to cookies, and somehow they look so much more appetizing to children than do the simple rounds.

Cookies are dainty and more delicate than cake, and can look particularly attractive served on an interesting dish. They can also make an imaginative gift, layered in a homemade box and tied with attractive ribbon. What better present could there be for a grandmother or aunt? Stored in an airtight container, most cookies will keep well for weeks.

This selection of recipes offers the traditional favorites as well as the more unusual varieties. Have fun selecting recipes, try baking your own cookies, and you'll soon discover just how delicious the results can be.

Walnut Raisin Cookies

MAKES 36 BISCUITS
Use your favorite dried fruit and nuts to vary these delicious cookies.

PREPARATION: 15 mins
COOKING: 8-10 mins

---

1 cup butter
1½ cups brown sugar
3 eggs
1 tsp baking soda dissolved in 1½ tbsps hot
    water
3¼ cups all-purpose flour, sifted
½ tsp salt
1 tsp cinnamon
⅔ cup walnuts, chopped
⅔ cup golden raisins

---

1. Cream the butter and sugar together in a mixing bowl until light and fluffy.

2. Beat in the eggs one at a time, beating well in between each addition.

3. Add the soda mixture, then work in half of the flour, together with the salt and cinnamon.

4. Mix in the walnuts and raisins, then the remaining flour.

5. Grease several baking trays and drop the mixture on by spoonfuls about 1 inch apart.

6. Bake in an oven preheated to 350°F about 8-10 minutes, or until golden-brown.

7. Remove from the trays with a metal spatula and cool on a wire rack.

Brown Sugar Cookies

MAKES ABOUT 36

These crisp cookies are perfect as an accompaniment to ice cream or fruit salad.

PREPARATION: 20 mins
COOKING: 10-12 mins

1¼ cups brown sugar
3 tbsps dark corn sirup
4 tbsps water
1 egg
1 cup all-purpose flour
1 tbsp ground ginger
1 tbsp baking soda
Pinch salt
4 tbsps finely chopped nuts

1. Mix the sugar, sirup, water, and egg together in a large bowl. Beat with an electric mixer until pale and thick.

2. Sift flour with the ginger, baking soda, and salt into the brown sugar mixture and add the nuts. Stir by hand until thoroughly mixed.

Step 3 Use a spoon to drop the mixture about 2 inches apart onto a greased baking tray.

3. Lightly oil three baking trays and drop the mixture on by spoonfuls about 2 inches apart.

4. Bake in an oven pre-heated to 375°F about 10-12 minutes, or until lightly browned around the edges. Leave on the baking tray 1-2 minutes before removing with a metal spatula to a wire rack to cool completely.

Step 1 Beat the sugar, sirup, water, and egg with an electric mixer until light.

Step 4 Bake until browned around the edges. Cool slightly and remove with a metal spatula.

Sand Cookies

MAKES 36

These lovely, rich cookies get their name from the French word "sable" meaning sand.

PREPARATION: 20 mins plus, chilling
COOKING: 10 mins

1 cup sugar
1 cup butter
1 egg, beaten
2 cups all-purpose flour
1 egg white, slightly beaten
Superfine sugar
Finely chopped pecans or walnuts

1. Cream the sugar and butter together until light and fluffy. Beat in the egg and gradually add the flour, working it in well to make a stiff dough. Not all the flour may be needed.

2. Chill the mixture overnight, or until firm enough to roll out. Roll the dough out in small portions on a well-floured surface. Cut into 2-3-inch circles with a cookie cutter.

3. Place on greased baking trays. Brush the tops with the beaten egg white and sprinkle with a mixture of sugar and finely chopped nuts.

4. Bake in an oven preheated to 350°F about 10 minutes, or until crisp and pale golden. Leave a few minutes on the baking trays then remove to wire cooling racks.

Pecan Pastries

MAKES 12

These sweet, nutty pastries are deep-fried to make them light and crisp.

PREPARATION: 30 mins
COOKING: 25 mins

1 cup all-purpose flour
1 tsp baking powder
¼ tsp salt
4 tbsps cold water
Oil for deep frying
1¼ cups dark corn sirup mixed with ⅔ cup molasses
3 tbsps finely chopped pecans

1. Sift the flour, baking powder, and salt together into a large bowl. Make a well in the center and add the cold water.

2. Using a wooden spoon, mix until a stiff dough forms, and then knead by hand until smooth.

Step 1 Sift the dry ingredients into a bowl and make a well in the center.

Step 3 On a floured surface, roll out each piece until very thin.

3. Divide the dough into 12 portions, each about the size of a walnut. Roll out each portion of dough on a floured surface until very thin.

4. Heat the oil in a deep-fat fryer to 350°F. Drop each piece of pastry into the hot fat using two forks. Twist the pastry just as it hits the oil. Cook one at a time until light brown.

5. In a large saucepan, boil the syrup until it reaches 239°F on a candy thermometer, or forms a soft ball when dropped into cold water.

6. Drain the pastries on kitchen paper after frying and dip carefully into the hot sirup. Sprinkle with pecans before the sirup sets, and allow to cool before serving.

Coconut Tiles

MAKES 30

These home-made cookies provide the perfect finishing touch to a wide variety of desserts, especially ice creams or water ices.

PREPARATION: 10 mins
COOKING: 35 mins

4 tbsps sugar
2 egg whites
½ cup all-purpose flour
½ cup butter, melted
3 tbsps shredded coconut

1. Beat the sugar into the egg whites. Add the flour and butter, beating well. Beat in the coconut, then allow to rest 10 minutes.

2. Butter 3 baking trays and use the back of a spoon to spread out 1 tbsp of mixture for each cookie.

3. Cook each batch 3-4 minutes in an oven

Step 3 Remove the cookies from the tray with a metal spatula.

preheated to 400°F. Remove the cookies from the trays with a metal spatula and immediately shape them around a rolling-pin. They will cool and harden very quickly. Slide onto a wire rack to cool.

4. Repeat the cooking and cooling operation until all the mixture has been used.

Step 2 Spread out about 1 tbsp of batter for each biscuit.

Step 3 Immediately shape the baked cookies around a rolling-pin.

Shortbread Cookies

MAKES ABOUT 18

Sandwich these biscuits together with raspberry jelly for children's parties.

PREPARATION: 10 mins
COOKING: 10-15 mins

1¼ cups all-purpose flour
⅓ cup light brown sugar, finely ground
½ cup soft margarine
½ tsp vanilla extract

1. Sift the flour and sugar together and rub in the margarine.

2. Add the vanilla extract and bind the mixture together.

3. Form into small balls and place on a baking tray a few inches apart.

4. With the back of a fork, flatten the balls, making a criss-cross pattern.

5. Bake in an oven preheated to 375°F about 10-15 minutes or until golden-brown in color.

6. Cool and store in an airtight container.

Macaroons

Serve these delicious chewy almond cookies with tea or coffee.

PREPARATION: 15 mins, plus 15 mins standing
COOKING: 15-20 mins

1½ cups whole almonds
1 cup sugar
2 egg whites

1. Blanch the almonds by plunging them into boiling water 2 minutes.

2. Skin the almonds and spread them over a baking tray.

3. Dry in a warm oven for a few minutes without browning.

4. Grind the sugar until it resembles superfine sugar.

5. Grind the almonds.

6. Sieve the sugar and almonds together.

7. In a large bowl, beat the egg whites until stiff but not dry.

8. Gradually fold in the almond and sugar mixture, using a metal tablespoon, and add the almond extract.

9. Pipe or spoon the mixture onto a floured baking tray, alternatively put spoonfuls of the mixture onto sheets of edible rice paper.

10. Leave 10-15 minutes to rest before baking.

11. Bake in an oven preheated to 350°F 15-20 minutes, or until golden-brown.

12. Transfer the cooked macaroons to a cooling rack.

Peanut Butter Bran Cookies

MAKES ABOUT 35

*These rich, crumbly cookies are just the thing for hungry kids, and make a good
mid-morning snack with a glass of milk.*

PREPARATION: 15 mins
COOKING: 10 mins

½ cup butter or margarine
½ cup light brown sugar
1 egg, beaten
1 cup crunchy peanut butter
½ cup bran
1 cup wholewheat flour
Pinch salt
½ tsp baking powder
½ tsp vanilla extract

1. Beat together the butter and sugar until pale

Step 2 Beat the peanut butter into the creamed mixture.

Step 2 Add the dry ingredients and vanilla to the peanut mixture, stirring well to make a stiff dough.

and creamy. Gradually add the egg, beating well after each addition.

2. Beat in the peanut butter, bran, flour, salt, baking powder, and vanilla, mixing well to form a stiff dough.

3. Take small pieces of the dough and roll into balls. Place well apart on two greased baking trays and flatten slightly with a fork or metal spatula.

4. Bake one tray at time, in an oven preheated to 375°F 5-10 minutes. Cool slightly on the tray, then transfer to a wire rack to cool completely.

Sunflower Chocolate Cookies

MAKES ABOUT 28

The addition of sunflower seeds to these cookies adds texture as well as a great flavor.

PREPARATION: 20 mins
COOKING: 10 mins

½ cup butter or margarine
½ cup light brown sugar
1 egg, beaten
1 tsp vanilla extract
½ tsp baking soda
½ tsp salt
2 tbsps bran
⅔ cup fine oatmeal
1 cup wholewheat flour
2 tbsps sunflower seeds
½ cup chocolate chips

1. Beat together the butter and sugar until pale and creamy. Gradually add the egg, beating well after each addition.

2. Beat in the vanilla extract, then beat in the baking soda, salt, bran, oats, and flour, mixing well until you have a stiff dough.

3. Finally, beat in the sunflower seeds and chocolate chips.

4. Place heaping spoonfuls of the mixture onto two greased baking trays and bake in an oven preheated to 375°F 5-10 minutes.

5. Cool slightly on the tray, then transfer to a wire rack to cool completely.

Granola Cookies

MAKES ABOUT 36

These simple-to-make cookies are full of wholesome ingredients.

PREPARATION: 15 mins
COOKING: 20 mins

½ cup butter or margarine
½ cup light brown sugar
1 egg, beaten
1 tsp vanilla extract
1 tsp baking powder
2 cups wholewheat flour
Pinch salt
1 cup granola
¼ cup currants

Step 2 Mix the dry ingredients and fruit into the egg mixture to form a stiff dough.

1. Beat together the butter and sugar until pale and creamy. Gradually add the egg, beating well after each addition.

2. Beat in the vanilla extract, then beat in the baking powder, flour, salt, granola, and currants to make a stiff dough.

3. Place heaping spoonfuls of the mixture onto two greased baking trays and bake in an oven preheated to 375°F 5-10 minutes.

4. Cool slightly on the tray then transfer to a wire rack to cool completely.

Lemon-Frosted Molasses Cookies

MAKES ABOUT 30

Children in particular will love these little cookies.

PREPARATION: 20 mins
COOKING: 30 mins

½ cup butter or margarine
½ cup light brown sugar
1 egg, beaten
2 tbsps blackstrap molasses
2 tsps baking powder
1 tsp ground allspice
½ tsp ground ginger
2 cups wholewheat flour
Pinch salt
8 cups powdered sugar
Grated rind and juice of 1 lemon
Yellow food coloring (optional)
Candied lemon slices (optional)
⅔ cup water

---

1. Beat together the butter and sugar until pale and creamy. Gradually add the egg, beating well after each addition.

2. Beat in the molasses, then using a metal spoon fold in the baking powder, spices, flour, and salt.

Step 1 Cream the sugar and butter together in a large bowl until they become fluffy and light in texture.

3. Place spoonfuls of the mixture onto two greased baking trays and bake one tray at a time 5-10 minutes in an oven preheated to 375°F.

4. Cool slightly on the tray then transfer to a wire rack to cool completely.

5. When all the cookies are baked, sift the powdered sugar into a bowl and add the lemon rind and juice. Add coloring, if using.

6. Gradually stir in enough water to form a thin frosting and spread equal amounts over each cookie. Decorate with candied lemon slices if wished, and allow the frosting to set before serving.

Langues de Chat

SERVES 6

"Cat's tongues" are a classic accompaniment to ice cream or fruit desserts, and are also traditionally served with afternoon tea.

PREPARATION: 15 mins
COOKING: 10-15 mins

⅔ cup softened butter
2 cups powdered sugar
1 tsp vanilla extract
5 egg whites
2 cups all-purpose flour, sifted

---

1. Cream the butter with the powdered sugar and the vanilla extract. Add the egg whites one by one, alternating with the flour, until a firm dough is obtained.

2. Place the dough in a piping bag fitted with a plain nozzle. Pipe even-sized strips of dough onto a greased baking tray. Leave space between the cookies, as they spread during baking.

Step 2 Spoon the cookie dough into a piping bag fitted with a plain nozzle.

Step 2 Pipe even-sized strips of dough onto a greased baking tray, leaving plenty of space between each.

3. Bake in an oven preheated to 400°F 10-15 minutes; the edges should be golden-brown but the centers still light.

4. When cooked, remove the cookies from the oven, allow them to cool slightly on the baking tray, then use a metal spatula to lift them onto a wire rack. Allow them to cool completely.

Step 4 When cooked and slightly cooled, remove the cookies to a cooling rack using a metal spatula.

Oatlet Cookies

MAKES 10

A delicious mix of oats, seeds, and sirup makes these cookies extra special.

PREPARATION: 15 mins
COOKING: 10 mins

---

1 cup raw coarse oatmeal
1 cup all-purpose flour
3 tbsps sunflower seeds
2 tbsps sesame seeds
½ tsp mixed spice
½ cup butter or margarine
1 tbsp brown sugar
1 tsp dark corn sirup or molasses
½ tsp baking powder
1 tbsp boiling water
1 cup chocolate pieces

---

1. Mix the oatmeal, flour, sunflower seeds, sesame seeds, and spice together.

2. Melt the butter, sugar and dark corn sirup or molasses over a gentle heat.

3. Add the baking powder and water to the sirup mixture and stir well.

4. Pour the dry ingredients over the butter mixture and mix well.

5. Place spoonfuls of the mixture well apart on a greased baking tray and bake in an oven preheated to 375°F 10 minutes.

6. Allow to cool on the tray.

7. Melt the chocolate pieces in a bowl over hot water and place teaspoonsful on top of the cookies. Leave to set. Store in an airtight tin.

Ginger Nuts

MAKES 36

These spicy cookies are given a delicious texture by including nuts in the recipe.

PREPARATION: 20 mins
COOKING: 10 mins

¾ cup butter or margarine
½ cup dark brown sugar
½ cup dark sirup
2 tsps vinegar
3 eggs, beaten
2 tbsps milk
6 cups wholewheat flour
1½ tsps baking soda
2 tsps ground ginger
½ tsp ground cinnamon
Pinch ground cloves
2 tbsps hazelnuts or walnuts, chopped

Step 1 Beat the butter, sugar, sirup, and vinegar together in a large bowl until they are smooth and well blended.

Step 2 Make a firm dough by beating the dry ingredients into the sirup mixture, and mixing well with a wooden spoon.

1. Put the butter, sugar, sirup, and vinegar into a large mixing bowl and beat together well until they are smooth and well blended.

2. Beat in the eggs and milk. Add the flour, baking soda, spices, and nuts, mixing well to form a firm dough.

3. Take small amounts of the cookie dough and roll into balls. Place well apart on two greased baking trays.

4. Press each cookie down with a fork and bake in an oven preheated to 375°F 5-10 minutes.

5. Cool slightly on the tray then transfer to a wire rack to cool completely.

Old-Fashioned Molasses Cookies

MAKES ABOUT 45

To make the preparation of these cookies easier, weigh the molasses directly into the saucepan.

PREPARATION: 10 mins
COOKING: 8-12 mins

⅔ cup sugar
¾ cup molasses
⅔ cup butter
⅔ cup buttermilk
3 cups all-purpose flour
1 tsp baking soda
2 tsps cinnamon
1 tsp ginger
½ tsp cloves
½ tsp nutmeg
½ tsp salt
¾ cup raisins, chopped

---

1. Place the sugar, molasses, and butter in a large, heavy-based pan and cook, stirring, until the mixture comes to the boil.

2. Allow to boil 1 minute, then remove from the heat and stir in the buttermilk.

3. Sift together the flour, baking soda, spices, and salt, and beat this thoroughly into the molasses mixture. Stir in the raisins.

4. Drop teaspoons of the mixture onto greased baking trays, leaving plenty of space between them, and bake in an oven preheated to 350°F 8-12 minutes.

5. When cooked, allow to cool slightly, before removing to a cake rack to cool completely.

Palmiers

These delicious flaky cookies originated in France. The name means "palm leaves."

PREPARATION: 15 mins, plus chilling
COOKING: 20 mins

---

8 ounces puff dough
3 tbsps superfine sugar
Powdered sugar

---

1. Roll the puff pastry out to form a rectangle 12 inches long and ⅛-inch thick.

2. Sprinkle a work surface with half the sugar. Place the dough on the sugared surface, and sprinkle with the remaining sugar. Roll the rolling-pin lightly over the dough so that the sugar sticks to the dough.

3. Roll each of the two short ends of the dough up toward the middle, and place the rolled dough in the freezer for 20 minutes, to make it easier to slice.

Step 3 Roll up the ends of the dough towards the middle.

4. Remove from the freezer and slice the rolled dough to the preferred thickness.

5. Place the cookies on a dampened baking tray. Bake in an oven preheated to 400°F 20 minutes, or until golden-brown.

6. Allow the palmiers to cool, then sprinkle with powdered sugar before serving.

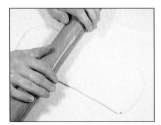

Step 1 Roll the dough out into a rectangle, about 12 inches long and ⅛ inch thick.

Step 4 Cut the chilled dough into slices.

Susan's Oaties

For a super taste add finely chopped nuts or shredded coconut to this recipe.

PREPARATION: 10 mins
COOKING: 20 mins

½ cup butter or margarine
½ cup brown sugar
1 tsp molasses
1 tsp boiling water
1 tsp baking soda
1 cup wholewheat flour
1 cup raw oatmeal
½ tsp baking powder

---

1. Melt the butter, sugar, and molasses in a saucepan.

2. Add the boiling water and baking soda.

3. Remove from the heat and stir in the flour, oatmeal and baking powder.

4. Place teaspoons of the mixture onto greased baking trays.

5. Bake in an oven preheated to 325°F 20 minutes.

6. Remove from the baking trays and place on a wire tray to cool.

Hermits

Replace the allspice and raisins with cinnamon and chopped nuts for a tasty variation.

PREPARATION: 15-20 mins
COOKING: 12-15 mins

½ cup butter
1 cup sugar
½ cup milk
2 cups all-purpose flour
1 tsp allspice
½ tsp baking soda
½ tsp cream of tartar
⅓ cup raisins

---

1. Cream the butter and sugar together until pale and fluffy, then gradually beat in the milk.

2. Sift together the flour, allspice, baking soda, and cream of tartar.

3. Add the flour mixture to the butter mixture, beating well after each addition until the mixture is smooth.

4. Chop the raisins and stir them into the mixture.

5. Drop teaspoons of the mixture onto greased baking trays, spacing them well apart.

6. Bake in an oven preheated to 375°F 12-15 minutes.

7. Allow to cool slightly before removing to a wire rack to cool completely.

Index